Credit Card Hacking for Smart Borrowers

By Joe Correa

Published by Live Stronger Faster

This book is for educational and informational purposes only. The author and publisher are not engaged in rendering legal, financial, or other professional advice. Readers should consult a qualified professional before making any financial decisions.

First Edition

Table of Contents

Chapter 1: The miles and points Wake-Up Call

Carlos had never flown first class before. In fact, he'd never flown without paying for checked luggage, fighting for armrest space, or worrying about the mounting credit card bills waiting at home. But there he was—seat 2A, sipping sparkling water, being offered a warm towel on his way to Hawaii—all thanks to a credit card welcome bonus he hadn't even known existed a year earlier.

Just twelve months ago, Carlos had been deep in debt, swiping cards for groceries and minimum payments. He had a decent job, sure, but every dollar seemed to vanish into rent, bills, and gas. Then, while watching a YouTube video on budgeting, he saw someone casually mention “credit card hacking.” At first, he scoffed. "Another scam," he thought.

But curiosity got the best of him. He spent that evening learning everything he could about points, sign-up bonuses, and how some people flew around the world for nearly free. The key? Strategic use of credit—not abuse. No debt. No gimmicks. Just leveraging what he already spent on bills and food to earn value back.

Carlos started with a basic cashback card—nothing fancy. Just

1.5% back on all purchases. But it was a win. He paid it off every two weeks, just like the tutorials recommended. No interest. No surprises.

Then he applied for a card offering 60,000 points after spending $4,000 in three months. At first, it seemed like a lot—but when he added his rent (paid via a fee-free rent portal), groceries, insurance, and utilities, he realized he already spent that much anyway. He just had to shift the payments to the card, without spending more.

That's when things changed.

With 60,000 points, Carlos booked two roundtrip flights to Mexico. He felt like he'd cracked some secret code. One that bankers don't teach you. One that your broke cousin doesn't know. One that most people use incorrectly—or not at all.

But Carlos wasn't done. He began learning about travel protections, free hotel nights, price protections, extended warranties, and rental car insurance—all included just for holding the right cards.

Now, Carlos teaches others. Friends, co-workers, even his parents. And he makes one rule very clear: **"If you can't pay the balance in full every month, don't play this game."**

This book is about unlocking the hidden wealth that credit

cards offer. Not by getting into debt—but by playing smart, spending intentionally, and paying it all off.

Chapter 2: Choosing the right cards for your goals

If you want to master credit card hacking, you need to start with the right foundation. That means choosing cards that align with your **financial behavior**, **credit score**, and personal goals. The mistake most people make? Chasing shiny rewards without a strategy—leading to unnecessary debt or underused perks. In this chapter, you'll learn how to select the ideal card for your unique goals and situation.

Step 1: Know Your Credit Score First

Before you apply for any credit card, pull your credit report and check your FICO score. You can do this for free using:

- AnnualCreditReport.com (for your full report from all three bureaus)
- Credit Karma or Credit Sesame (for educational scores and monitoring)
- Or your bank's built-in credit tracker

Why it matters: Each credit card has a recommended score range. If your score is too low, you'll get denied—and each denial can temporarily lower your score further due to the hard inquiry.

Target Ranges:

- Excellent Credit (750+): Access to premium travel cards, elite cashback cards, and business cards
- Good Credit (700–749): Solid travel and cashback options with decent bonuses
- Fair Credit (640–699): Consider starter cards or secured cards with rewards
- Poor Credit (<640): Focus first on rebuilding your credit before chasing rewards

Step 2: Define Your Reward Strategy

Ask yourself: *What do I want from this card?* Your answer should shape the type of card you apply for. The three main categories are:

1. **Travel Rewards**
    - Earn points or miles you can redeem for flights, hotels, car rentals, or upgrades.
    - Ideal for people who travel a few times a year or want to plan free vacations.

2. **Cashback**
    - Earn a percentage of your purchases back in cash (usually 1.5%–5%).
    - Best for people who want simple, flexible rewards they can use on anything.
3. **Balance Transfers or Low-Interest Intro Offers**
    - Useful for those who need to pay off existing debt and avoid interest.

Example:

- If you spend heavily on groceries and gas: look for a **card with 3%–6% cashback in those categories.**
- If you travel frequently: look for a **card with airline partners, free checked bags, and airport lounge access.**

Step 3: Understand the Fees and Interest Rates

Even great rewards cards can have hidden downsides. Always check the **Annual Percentage Rate (APR)** and **fees** before applying.

Key fees to look for:

- **Annual Fee:** Some travel and cashback cards charge $95–$695 per year. Make sure your rewards exceed this.

- **Foreign Transaction Fees:** If you travel abroad, look for a card with *0% foreign transaction fees.*

- **Balance Transfer Fees:** If transferring debt, check for a **0% APR promo** and **3% or lower transfer fee.**

Warning: If you **don't pay your balance in full**, your interest charges can wipe out all rewards. Credit card hacking only works when you're paying off the card **monthly, in full.**

Step 4: Find the Best Welcome Bonuses

One of the fastest ways to earn travel and cashback value is through **welcome bonuses**, sometimes called **sign-up bonuses**.

Typical Offer: Spend $3,000 in the first 3 months and get 60,000 points or $500 cash back.

This can be worth hundreds—or even thousands—when redeemed for flights or hotels.

Pro Tip: Make sure the **minimum spend requirement** matches your normal spending. Never spend more just to meet a bonus—it defeats the purpose.

Step 5: Consider Long-Term Value

Beyond the initial bonus, consider the **ongoing rewards** and perks that fit your lifestyle:

- **Rotating Categories:** Cards like the Chase Freedom Flex offer 5% cashback on changing categories each quarter.
- **Flat Rate Cards:** Like the Citi Double Cash (2% on everything).
- **Premium Travel Cards:** Like the Chase Sapphire Preferred or Amex Gold, which come with travel insurance, priority boarding, and more.

Additional Perks to Look For:

- Cell phone protection
- Extended warranties
- Price protection
- Return protection

- Rental car insurance

If these perks match your habits, they add even more value.

Step 6: Apply Smart—One Card at a Time

Space out your applications. Too many at once can:

- Lower your score due to multiple hard inquiries
- Get you denied for appearing "credit hungry"

Rule of Thumb: Apply for **one new card every 3–6 months**, unless you're following an advanced strategy like the "Chase 5/24 Rule" (which we'll cover later in the book).

Summary Action Plan

1. **Check your credit score and reports**
2. **Define your goals: travel, cashback, or balance transfer**
3. **Compare cards by rewards, fees, and long-term benefits**
4. **Plan for the welcome bonus by aligning it with normal expenses**

5. **Apply when your score is ready and your spending aligns**

By choosing the right card with strategy, not impulse, you set yourself up for long-term financial wins—whether it's free flights, cashback, or smarter credit building.

The Story of Maya's Financial Transformation

Maya had always been careful with her money. As a middle school teacher in Georgia, she lived modestly, saved when she could, and avoided credit cards like they were traps. She'd grown up watching her parents struggle with debt—late-night calls from collectors, overdraft notices on the fridge, and holidays filled with stress instead of joy. To Maya, credit cards represented everything she didn't want to become.

But things changed when Maya turned 30. She wanted more freedom—to travel, to see her family in California without draining her savings, to stop feeling like she had to choose between an oil change and a weekend getaway. That's when she heard about "credit card hacking" on a podcast while grading essays. At first, she rolled her eyes. But something about the guest's story caught her attention.

This woman, also a teacher, had flown to Europe twice in one year—just by using points. No gimmicks. No interest. Just strategic credit use. Maya paused the podcast and started searching. "Is credit card hacking legit?" "How do I start travel hacking?" She stayed up until 2 a.m. reading blogs, YouTube guides, and Reddit threads.

By the next morning, she was ready to try. But Maya didn't just jump in. She made a list of her goals:

1. Fly to California twice a year to visit her parents
2. Stay in hotels without breaking her budget
3. Get cashback on groceries and school supplies

She realized she wasn't looking for luxury—she just wanted value. So she started with her credit score: 728. Not bad. She qualified for most cards, which meant she had options. But that also made the decision harder.

Maya made a spreadsheet and categorized cards into three groups: travel, cashback, and balance transfer. She narrowed it down to two choices:

- **The Chase Sapphire Preferred**, offering 60,000 points after $4,000 in spending
- **The Amex Blue Cash Preferred**, offering 6% cashback on groceries and streaming

She hesitated. The Sapphire card came with a $95 annual fee and seemed focused on serious travelers. The Amex had more practical benefits for her daily life.

Then she had an idea: why not plan a strategy that combined both? She'd start with the cashback card to earn rewards on her daily spending, and later, once she had a rhythm, she'd go for the travel card.

Maya applied for the Amex Blue Cash Preferred. She was approved instantly. Limit: $5,000. She took a deep breath. "Okay," she told herself. "I'm going to use this the right way."

She automated her bill payments and groceries onto the card. Every Sunday night, she paid off the balance with the money she had already set aside. No stress. No temptation. Just a system.

Three months later, she had earned over $300 in cashback and had paid **zero** in interest. That summer, she used her rewards to cover a hotel for a three-night stay in Savannah. Her first "free" vacation. She was hooked.

By the next year, she added the Chase Sapphire Preferred to her wallet. She put her annual insurance, back-to-school expenses, and holiday travel on the card—all things she already planned to buy. She hit the $4,000 bonus mark with ease and used the points to fly to San Diego in December.

On that flight, window seat, headphones in, Maya smiled. She wasn't rich. She hadn't gotten a raise. But she felt powerful.

She had learned how to use credit on her terms. No fear. No shame. Just strategy.

Now she teaches others. Her friends at work, her brother, even a few of her students' parents. "The trick isn't just using credit," she says. "It's choosing the right card for your life—not someone else's."

Maya now reviews her cards every six months. She cancels ones she no longer uses, applies for new ones when the bonuses make sense, and always—always—pays in full.

And the best part? She finally bought her parents flights to come visit her for Thanksgiving. She used her points to cover everything. No debt. No guilt. Just joy.

Chapter 3: Earning and Maximizing Rewards Daily

Once you've chosen the right credit card, the next step is learning how to use it **strategically and consistently** to earn maximum rewards. This chapter will teach you exactly how to turn everyday spending into free flights, hotel stays, cashback, and more—**without spending a penny more than you already do.**

If you do this right, your credit cards become **income-producing tools**, not expenses.

Step 1: Organize Your Spending Into Reward Categories

Every credit card offers different rewards depending on where and how you spend money. Start by creating a **spending map** of your top 5 expense categories. Here's how:

Example: Maya's Monthly Spending Map

- Groceries: $450
- Gas: $150
- Streaming Subscriptions: $60
- Dining Out: $200

- Utilities and Insurance: $300
- Other: $100

Once you know where your money goes, **match those categories** to the right card. For example:

- Use a card with 6% cashback on groceries for your supermarket purchases.
- Use a card with 3x or 5x points on dining for restaurants.
- Use a flat-rate 2% cashback card for non-category purchases.

This matching process is called **"category alignment."** Most people never do it, and they leave hundreds—if not thousands—of dollars in rewards on the table.

Step 2: Stack Bonuses with Portals, Offers, and Extensions

Now that your categories are matched, you can **stack rewards** to increase earnings without changing what you buy.

Three Easy Ways to Stack:

1. **Online Shopping Portals** – Use portals like Rakuten, TopCashback, or your credit card issuer's

portal (e.g., Chase Ultimate Rewards or Amex Offers). You click through the portal before buying from major retailers like Nike, Walmart, or Best Buy and earn **additional cashback or points.**

2. **Card-linked Offers** – Activate targeted offers through your bank. For example, Amex Offers might give you $20 back for spending $100 at a certain store.

3. **Browser Extensions** – Install tools like *Honey*, *Capital One Shopping*, or *Rakuten* that alert you to coupon codes and cash bonuses while browsing.

Example: Maya buys a $100 pair of running shoes from Nike:

- Uses Chase Sapphire Preferred (3x points on travel & certain online purchases)
- Clicks through Rakuten for 8% cashback
- Activates a $10 cashback offer through her card's app

Result: $8 cashback + 300 Chase points + $10 bonus = triple-stacked rewards

Step 3: Automate and Optimize Your Bill Payments

Bills are a credit card hacker's secret weapon. Most people pay them through their bank account and earn **nothing**. But when possible, pay bills through your credit card to:

- Hit spending thresholds for welcome bonuses
- Earn rewards on regular fixed costs

Bills You Can Often Put on Credit Cards:

- Phone, internet, and streaming
- Insurance (home, auto, life)
- Utilities (with payment processors like Plastiq)
- Subscriptions (software, gym, cloud storage)

Warning: Never pay rent, mortgage, or taxes with a credit card unless:

- The fee is under 2.5% AND
- You're hitting a big bonus AND
- You'll pay it off in full the same month

Step 4: Take Advantage of Monthly Perks and Credits

Premium cards often offer **credits and protections** most cardholders forget to use. These are automatic money-savers.

Examples of Common Credits:

- Amex Gold: $10/month dining credit (Uber Eats, Grubhub)
- Chase Sapphire Reserve: $300 annual travel credit
- Hilton Aspire: $250 airline fee credit + free hotel night

How to Maximize: Set a **monthly reminder** to use credits. Consider keeping a running list in your Notes app or calendar for:

- Monthly statement credits
- Free shipping perks
- Priority access or reservations

If you're not using these perks, you're not getting the full value of the card—and in most cases, you're losing money on the annual fee.

Step 5: Track, Review, and Adjust Every Quarter

Every three months, conduct a **card performance review**. Ask:

- Which cards gave me the most rewards?
- Did I use them in the right categories?
- Did I miss any bonus offers or credits?
- Are there better options I should consider switching to?

Use tools like:

- **Mint** or **YNAB** to track expenses by category
- **AwardWallet** or **MaxRewards** to track points and offers
- **Google Sheets** for a custom tracker of all your card benefits, bonuses, and due dates

Example Review Summary:

- Amex Blue Cash: $72 in grocery cashback (6%)
- Chase Freedom Flex: $54 from Q1 rotating category (gas)

- Amex Offers: $20 from Staples credit
- Rakuten: $45 cashback from portal stacking

Total reward value this quarter: $191

Final Tips for Everyday Reward Mastery

1. **Never use a debit card unless absolutely necessary.** Debit gives you zero rewards and less protection.
2. **Pay your balance every week, not just every month.** It keeps your credit utilization low and protects your score.
3. **Avoid carrying more than 2–3 active cards** if you're just starting. Focus on what you can manage easily and responsibly.
4. **Treat points and cashback like real money.** Because they are—when used wisely.

Chapter Recap:

- Match your credit cards to your top spending categories
- Stack rewards through portals, offers, and apps
- Put recurring bills on your cards to boost passive points

- Use every monthly perk and credit you're entitled to
- Review your usage every quarter to optimize earnings

This chapter is about building habits. You don't need to chase the next shiny card—you just need to **use what you have smartly and consistently.**

The Story of Derek, the Daily Hacker

Derek Alvarez had never considered himself the "organized" type. He was a freelance graphic designer in Austin, Texas, juggling multiple clients, chasing down invoices, and keeping up with software subscriptions, groceries, and bills. His finances were more like organized chaos—until a random YouTube rabbit hole one evening introduced him to the world of credit card rewards.

At first, it sounded like a rich person's game—first class flights, airport lounges, luxury hotels. "Must be nice," he thought. But as he dug deeper, he discovered people like him—regular folks—who were earning hundreds, even thousands of dollars in travel and cashback every year just by using their credit cards **intentionally**.

He didn't need luxury. What he wanted was **efficiency**. To stop feeling like every dollar disappeared the second he earned it. To use the spending he already had to his advantage.

So he took a deep breath and decided to try. One rule: he would never carry a balance. Not a penny.

Derek started by mapping out his expenses. He opened up his budgeting app and looked at the last 3 months:

- Food delivery and dining out: $600/month
- Subscriptions and software: $300/month
- Gas and rideshares: $200/month
- Groceries: $250/month
- Miscellaneous (client gifts, office supplies, and tech): $150/month

"Okay," he thought. "Now what?"

He read that the **Amex Gold Card** offered 4x points on dining and supermarkets. That seemed perfect. He applied—and got approved. Next, he picked up the **Chase Freedom Flex**, which offered 5% cashback in rotating categories, and the **Citi Double Cash** for a flat 2% back on everything else.

For the first time in his adult life, Derek felt like he had a **system**.

He color-coded his cards with tiny stickers—red for Amex (dining and groceries), green for Citi (everything else), and blue for Chase (rotating categories). He even created a digital cheat sheet on his phone labeled "What Card to Use Where."

Soon, things got fun.

One morning, he ordered lunch through Uber Eats using his Amex Gold. He remembered he had activated an Amex Offer for $10 back on a $25 Uber Eats purchase. The food cost $28. He got 112 points for the purchase—**and** $10 instantly credited back to his account.

Another time, while buying software for a client project, he checked the Rakuten portal. Adobe was offering **8% cashback** if you clicked through Rakuten first. He did, made the $100 purchase, and got $8 back in his Rakuten account—on top of the 2% he'd earn with his Citi card.

His favorite moment came three months in. Derek looked at his Chase and Amex accounts and saw:

- **Amex Membership Rewards points: 34,000**
- **Chase Ultimate Rewards: 16,200**
- **Cashback earned on Citi: $92**

That was over **$600 in travel or cash**—earned without changing his lifestyle at all.

He hadn't spent more. He hadn't done anything complicated. He'd just aligned his spending to the right cards.

Then came the big test: Derek planned a weekend trip to Denver with friends. He checked his points, transferred Amex rewards to Delta, and booked a roundtrip flight worth $362. The cost to him? $0.

He sat on the plane, boarding group one, sipping coffee. "This is nuts," he said to himself. "I'm flying for free because I bought groceries and paid for Netflix."

Now, he was obsessed—in a good way.

He created a spreadsheet that tracked every card's category bonuses, expiration dates, credit limits, and perks. He scheduled a monthly 15-minute "reward check-in" on the first Sunday of each month.

He made it a game: **How much free value can I squeeze from the money I already spend?**

But Derek was also smart. He never used his cards to buy things he couldn't afford. He never paid interest. He used autopay, reminders, and set all his cards to alert him when his balance reached 50%.

It wasn't just about the points anymore. It was about control. Clarity. Ownership of his financial life.

By the end of the year, Derek had earned:

- Two roundtrip flights
- Three hotel nights at a Marriott
- $200 in cashback
- A year's worth of Adobe Creative Cloud for free using Amex Offers
- And his credit score? It jumped from 712 to 761.

All because he used the **same money he'd always spent**—but ran it through a smarter system.

Now, his friends come to him for advice. He teaches them how to pick the right card, how to use browser extensions, and how to review their cards quarterly.

But his advice always starts the same:

> "Don't start with travel. Start with groceries, gas, and Netflix. Start with what you're already doing. Master that. And never carry a balance."

Derek may not have been organized at first, but now he's a **daily hacker**—someone who earns while they live, saves while they spend, and travels while others say, "I wish I could afford that."

Chapter 4: Redeeming Rewards the Smart Way

Earning points, miles, or cashback is only half the game. The real value of credit card hacking comes when you **redeem those rewards wisely**. Redeeming without a strategy can cut their value in half—or worse, waste them entirely. This chapter will show you how to turn your hard-earned points into real value for **travel, cashback, gift cards, or experiences**, all while avoiding common redemption traps.

Step 1: Understand Reward Values and Their Hidden Math

Each reward system works differently, and not all points are created equal. Let's look at three types:

1. **Cashback** – Usually fixed value:
    - 1% = $0.01 per dollar spent
    - 5% = $0.05 per dollar spent This is the most straightforward redemption.
2. **Travel Points (Flexible Programs)** – Such as Chase Ultimate Rewards, Amex Membership Rewards, and Citi ThankYou Points:
    - Value can vary: **$0.01 to $0.025** per point

  - Better redemptions come from **transfer partners** (airlines, hotels)

3. **Airline Miles or Hotel Points** – Each has its own system:
   - Delta SkyMiles: ~$0.012 per mile (but varies)
   - Marriott Bonvoy: ~$0.007 per point The key is finding **sweet spots**, which we'll explain shortly.

Step 2: Avoid Low-Value Redemption Traps

Credit card issuers often tempt users with easy options that sound good—but offer **poor value**. Examples:

- **Gift cards**: Often redeem at 0.8 to 1 cent per point
- **Merchandise or shopping portals**: Extremely poor value (0.5 to 0.8 cents per point)
- **"Pay With Points" at checkout (e.g., Amazon)**: Usually gives the **worst** rate—sometimes less than 0.7 cents per point

Rule of Thumb: If it's convenient, it probably comes with **less value**. Take the extra step to transfer or redeem your points properly—it can **double or triple your reward value**.

Step 3: Redeem Travel Rewards the Right Way

The best value often comes from transferring your flexible points (Chase, Amex, Citi) to airline or hotel partners.

Examples:

- **Chase Ultimate Rewards → Hyatt**: Book luxury hotels for a fraction of the points compared to using the Chase portal.
- **Amex Membership Rewards → ANA or Air Canada**: Fly roundtrip to Europe or Asia for 60k–80k points, when direct purchases would cost $1,000+.
- **Citi ThankYou Points → Turkish Airlines**: Fly U.S. to Hawaii for 15k miles roundtrip—an incredible deal.

These are called **sweet spots**, and they make your points go much further.

Steps to Transfer:

1. Log into your credit card rewards portal.

2. Choose your airline/hotel transfer partner.
3. Link your loyalty account (e.g., Marriott Bonvoy, Delta SkyMiles).
4. Transfer the required number of points.
5. Book through the airline or hotel's platform, not your card issuer's site.

Warning: Transfers are often **non-reversible** and can take 1–5 days, so always confirm availability before initiating a transfer.

Step 4: Use Travel Portals for Simplicity and Solid Value

If transferring points feels overwhelming, don't worry—you can still get decent value through your card's travel portal.

Chase Example:

- Chase Sapphire Preferred gives you **25% more value** when booking through the Chase Travel Portal.
    - 60,000 points = $750 in travel (instead of $600 cash)

How to Use It:

- Search for flights, hotels, or rental cars through your bank's travel portal (like Expedia or Priceline).
- Use your points at a fixed enhanced rate (e.g., 1.25 cents or 1.5 cents per point).
- You often earn miles and elite credits on these bookings, unlike with point transfers.

This is a great middle-ground for people who want **simplicity** with **above-average value**.

Step 5: Combine Points, Pool Rewards, and Redeem as a Team

Most people don't know that you can often combine or share points with spouses, business partners, or family members.

Chase:

- Combine points from all your Chase cards to maximize value (e.g., Freedom + Sapphire Preferred = higher redemption power)
- Transfer points to one household member per policy

Amex & Citi:

- Allow transfers to authorized users or linked loyalty accounts

Pro Tip: Designate one person as the "redemption strategist" in your household. Pool points into that account for large bookings or high-value redemptions.

Step 6: Redeem Cashback the Right Way

Cashback cards don't offer travel transfers, but they still need strategy.

Best Practices:

- **Redeem for statement credits or direct deposit**, not gift cards
- **Wait until larger balances** to avoid friction or fees
- Use cashback for **specific goals** like emergency funds, debt payoffs, or reinvestment in other tools (like paying for your next course or software)

Stack Your Strategy:

- Use cashback from one card to pay an annual fee on a travel card
- Use your rewards to offset costs of side hustle investments

- Combine with bank bonuses or referral rewards for extra income

Chapter Summary and Action Plan

To redeem rewards the smart way:

1. **Know the true value** of your points, miles, or cashback.
2. **Avoid poor redemption options** like gift cards or Amazon checkouts.
3. **Transfer points to airline/hotel partners** when seeking maximum value.
4. **Use portals like Chase Travel or Amex Travel** when seeking simplicity and decent value.
5. **Combine points within households or among your own cards** to boost redemption power.
6. **Cashback works best when used with intention**, not for impulse spending.

Redemption is the **payoff** phase of credit card hacking. The smarter you are here, the higher your return on every dollar you spend.

The Story of Amanda's Upgrade

Amanda Douglas had always been the type to collect things—coins, postcards, airline miles. But collecting points from credit cards? That was something she'd been doing for years without actually using them. Like digital trophies, they sat untouched in her account, gathering virtual dust.

She'd opened her first travel rewards card, the Chase Sapphire Preferred, three years ago when she got a promotion as a marketing coordinator. She earned the welcome bonus—60,000 points—and told herself she'd use them for a dream vacation someday. Then life happened.

Someday became next year. Next year became never.

By the time Amanda turned 35, she had **over 210,000 points** across Chase, Amex, and Citi cards. She had no idea what they were worth, how to use them, or where to start. She'd redeemed some for gift cards here and there—$50 to Amazon, $100 to Target—but it never felt exciting. It felt... average.

Then, her younger brother Jason booked a $4,000 roundtrip flight to Japan using just 70,000 points. First class. Private suite. Free meals and drinks. No cash. Amanda stared at the photos he sent from the ANA lounge in Tokyo and felt a wave of regret.

"You used points for that?" she asked, shocked.

"Of course," he laughed. "What else are they for?"

That was her wake-up call.

Amanda opened her laptop that night and logged into her Chase account. She clicked "Redeem Points," and sure enough, the first thing she saw was "$0.01 per point" for gift cards. A $100 Visa card would cost her 10,000 points.

"But Jason booked a first-class ticket for 70,000 points," she thought. "That's worth four grand. That's like... 6 cents per point?"

She did the math again. Her stomach dropped. She'd traded her valuable points for store credit. Over and over.

"I've been doing this all wrong."

She dove headfirst into travel hacking forums, YouTube guides, and Reddit posts. She learned about **sweet spots**—those rare redemptions where your points stretch farther than you'd think. Like booking Hyatt hotels through Chase, or transferring Amex points to Air Canada for flights to Europe.

She learned how **gift cards and Amazon checkouts are the worst redemptions**, how **travel portals give better value**, and how **airline transfers can explode the value of her points—if she plays it right.**

And she was ready to play.

Her next trip was to New York for a marketing conference. She found a Hyatt hotel near the venue: $480 per night. But through Chase's portal? Just 18,000 points per night. Four nights. 72,000 points total.

She clicked "Book." Boom. $1,920 in hotel value—redeemed for points.

Then came the flight. Delta was charging $350 one way. But she remembered Amex points could transfer to Air France and book Delta flights through their SkyTeam partnership.

After a few searches, she found it: JFK to ATL, roundtrip, 24,000 Amex points + $11 in taxes.

She transferred the points instantly. Five minutes later, the flight was booked.

"Okay," she whispered to herself. "That's $2,270 in travel for less than 100,000 points."

And she still had over 100,000 points left.

Amanda kept going. She made a chart in Google Sheets with each of her cards, their point balances, and the best transfer partners. She learned that her **Chase Freedom Flex points could be moved to her Sapphire account**, giving them more power when redeemed through the Chase Travel Portal. She even taught her coworker how to book a honeymoon using only points.

But the real reward came in April.

Amanda had always dreamed of going to Italy. But she'd assumed it was too expensive. With her new skills, she searched award travel sites and found a roundtrip business-class ticket from Boston to Rome on United—through a Chase transfer partner—for 80,000 points.

She booked it.

The day she boarded, sipping champagne in the Polaris Lounge, she smiled.

She had spent the same money she always did—on groceries, business lunches, software subscriptions—but this time, she'd **redeemed it with intention**.

She now saw her credit cards not as bills, but as tools. Tools that paid her to live her life smarter.

As the flight attendant offered her a hot towel, Amanda thought back to those $50 gift cards. She almost laughed. Those were scraps.

This... this was the **real** value of credit.

And she'd only just begun.

Chapter 5: Managing Multiple Cards Like a Pro

Once you've mastered earning and redeeming rewards from a single card, the natural next step is expanding your strategy. But with more cards comes more complexity—and more opportunity. This chapter teaches you how to manage multiple credit cards **without missing payments, damaging your credit, or getting overwhelmed**—all while maximizing every dollar you spend.

Step 1: Know Why You're Adding a New Card

Before you add a second, third, or fourth card, be clear about your goal. Each card in your wallet should serve a **specific purpose**.

Here are smart reasons to open a new card:

- To **earn a welcome bonus**
- To **unlock category-specific rewards** (like 5% on groceries or gas)
- To **access travel perks** (airport lounges, free hotel nights, priority boarding)
- To **increase your available credit** and lower your

credit utilization ratio

Avoid applying out of FOMO or to cover emergency expenses. Cards are tools—not crutches.

Step 2: Build a System to Keep Track of Everything

As you add cards, staying organized becomes essential. A forgotten payment or misunderstood benefit can wipe out months of progress.

Create a Credit Card Tracker that includes:

- **Card name and issuer**
- **Open date**
- **Credit limit**
- **Due date**
- **Current balance**
- **Rewards type** (points, miles, cashback)
- **Annual fee and when it's due**
- **Category bonuses and perks**
- **Welcome bonus and spend deadline (if new)**

You can use:

- A simple spreadsheet (Google Sheets works well)
- Free apps like **MaxRewards**, **AwardWallet**, or **Travel Freely**
- Reminder apps or calendar alerts for payment due dates

Pro Tip: Color-code your categories and rotate your focus every 90 days based on new promotions, limited-time offers, or bonus categories.

Step 3: Set Up Autopay—and Check Weekly Anyway

The golden rule of credit card hacking: **never carry a balance**.

Set up **autopay** for the full statement balance for every card. That way, even if you forget, you won't pay interest.

However, don't just "set and forget."

Instead:

- **Check your balances weekly** to ensure no fraudulent charges have appeared
- Pay off your balance **early** if you want to keep your credit utilization ratio low

- Log expenses into your budget so you don't overspend just to chase rewards

Even experienced users get tripped up when they don't monitor closely.

Step 4: Use the Right Card in the Right Place

This is where the magic happens: aligning your spending with the **highest-earning card** for that specific purchase.

Here's a breakdown of how a 3-card user might do it:

Expense Type	Best Card Example	Why Use It?
Dining & Takeout	Amex Gold (4x points)	Highest rate for restaurants
Groceries	Blue Cash Preferred (6% cashback)	Best return on food
Gas & Transit	Chase Freedom Flex (5% quarterly)	Rotating bonus category
Streaming Services	Citi Custom Cash (5% in top category)	Matches top spend category monthly
Online Shopping	Rakuten Portal + any rewards card	Stack cashback and card points
Travel	Chase Sapphire Preferred (2x travel)	Plus 25% bonus when redeemed

Pro Tip: Use stickers, digital wallet notes, or custom card names on Apple Pay/Google Pay to remind yourself of the card's category bonuses.

Step 5: Review Cards and Benefits Quarterly

Every 3 months, do a credit card checkup:

- Are you still using the card enough to justify the **annual fee**?
- Are you using all the included **credits and benefits**?
- Are any **bonus categories changing** soon?
- Are there new **welcome offers** you could qualify for?

If a card no longer serves a purpose:

- **Call the issuer** and ask if you can **product change** to a no-fee version
- Downgrade instead of closing the card to preserve your credit history

Why this matters: Length of credit history and total available credit are major factors in your credit score. Don't lose years of progress just because you're not using a card daily.

Step 6: Protect Yourself from Fraud and Identity Theft

The more cards you have, the more vigilant you must be.

Best Practices:

- Set up **text or email alerts** for every transaction
- Use **virtual card numbers** when shopping online (offered by Capital One, Citi, and others)
- Freeze cards you don't use often through your bank's app
- Check your **credit reports monthly** with services like Credit Karma or Experian

If fraud is detected:

- Report it immediately to your card issuer
- File a report with the FTC at **identitytheft.gov**
- Monitor your credit for new inquiries or accounts

Staying proactive keeps your financial identity secure while you build wealth through smart credit use.

Chapter 5 Recap: Your Multi-Card Management Plan

1. **Add cards with a specific strategy**—don't collect them aimlessly.
2. **Track all your cards** with a spreadsheet or app—know your limits, bonuses, and due dates.
3. **Set up autopay** but still monitor activity weekly.
4. **Match spending to the right card**—use every card where it earns the most.
5. **Review your lineup quarterly**—maximize value or downgrade dead weight.
6. **Stay secure**—enable alerts, use virtual cards, and monitor credit reports regularly.

With a little structure and strategy, managing multiple cards isn't stressful—it's empowering. It transforms you from a passive consumer into an intentional earner. The more cards you manage well, the more free flights, cashback, and opportunities flow your way.

The Story of Malik's Card Control

Malik Summers had a system for everything—his calendar, his fitness goals, even the order of spices in his kitchen. But when it came to credit cards, his system was chaos.

He had seven cards. One in his wallet, two in a drawer, one in his glove compartment for gas, and three more that he couldn't even remember applying for. Malik was good with money—he never missed a payment—but he was **leaving thousands of dollars in rewards on the table** every year.

It hit him one afternoon at his favorite coffee shop. He swiped a card for his $5 flat white, and his friend Chris shook his head.

"Dude... you just used a 1% cashback card at a restaurant. Why not 4x points?"

Malik laughed it off, but when he got home, he pulled out all his cards and laid them on the dining table like a poker hand. Chase Sapphire Preferred, Amex Blue Cash, Citi Double Cash, Target REDcard, an Amazon Visa, Discover It, and something called the HSBC Platinum Rewards that he hadn't touched since college.

He felt like a magician who didn't know his own tricks.

That night, Malik made a promise to himself: **no more wasted potential**. He would create a real system. Something scalable. Something that fit his brain the way his gym split or his Google Calendar did.

Step one: a spreadsheet.

He opened Excel and built a table:

- Card name
- Issuer
- Category bonuses
- Credit limit
- Payment due date
- Annual fee
- Notes and perks

As he filled in the columns, patterns emerged. He realized his Chase Sapphire gave him 2x points on dining and travel—but he'd been using his Citi Double Cash (2% flat rate) for everything out of habit. His Amex gave him 6% cashback at grocery stores, but he never brought it to Publix. And the Amazon card? Great for Amazon. But he rarely shopped there anymore.

He color-coded each card by category:

- **Green for groceries**
- **Blue for travel and dining**
- **Yellow for gas and transit**
- **Red for online shopping**
- **Gray for storage or backup**

Then came the real challenge: **payment dates**. They were all over the place. One was due on the 2nd, another on the 11th, two on the 20th, and one randomly on the 27th.

Malik called each bank and requested the same due date: the 15th. Most of them agreed. Now, instead of chasing bills all month, he had a single "credit card check-in" day—set on the second Sunday of every month. It was sacred.

Step two: automation.

He set every card to **autopay the full statement balance**. No interest. No surprises. But he didn't stop there. He added weekly calendar reminders to:

- Check balances
- Log any unexpected charges

- Adjust his spending if a card was getting too close to the limit

Step three: practice.

He started small. For one week, he made it a game: use only the card that earned the **most** rewards for that specific purchase. Groceries? Amex. Dining? Sapphire. Gas? Discover It's 5% category for Q2. Everything else? Citi Double Cash.

By day three, it was second nature. He even renamed the cards in his Apple Wallet to say **"Dining Only," "Groceries Only,"** and **"Everything Else."**

Soon, he wasn't just managing his cards—he was **mastering them.**

But the real payoff came six months later.

Malik had been tracking his rewards in the same spreadsheet. He tallied up the results:

- $122 in cashback from Amex
- $134 in Ultimate Rewards from Chase, worth $167 in travel
- $84 from Discover's quarterly bonuses

- $220 in cashback from Citi
- A $100 Amazon gift card from his Visa

Total reward value: **$727.**

He hadn't changed his income. He hadn't bought anything he wouldn't have bought anyway. He just used the right card in the right place, and he never paid a cent in interest.

It felt like getting a raise—quietly, automatically, without asking.

Later that year, Malik took a trip to San Diego. Flights and hotel? Booked with points. Rental car? Paid with cashback. Dinner with friends on the beach? Chase Sapphire. Double points, thank you.

Now, when his friends ask about his system, he pulls up the spreadsheet with a grin. "I treat my credit cards like employees," he says. "Each one has a role. If it's not doing its job, it gets demoted."

Malik didn't just learn how to manage multiple cards—he turned them into a **money-making machine**. And like everything else in his life, it runs on a system.

Chapter 6: The Secrets to Building Credit While Hacking Rewards

If you want to master credit card hacking long-term, you must understand how to **build and protect your credit score** while earning rewards. Many people focus on points and cashback but forget the foundational system that makes this strategy possible: a strong credit profile.

This chapter will teach you how to **boost your score, avoid damaging mistakes, and use credit cards to your advantage without hurting your future borrowing power**.

Step 1: Understand What Makes Up Your Credit Score

There are five key factors that affect your FICO score, which most lenders use to evaluate your creditworthiness:

1. **Payment History (35%)**
    - Do you pay on time? Every time?
    - Missing a payment can stay on your report for **7 years**.
2. **Credit Utilization (30%)**

- This is the percentage of your available credit that you're using.
- Aim to use **under 30%**, and ideally under **10%** on each card and overall.

3. **Length of Credit History (15%)**
   - Older accounts = stronger score. Don't close your oldest cards unless absolutely necessary.
4. **New Credit Inquiries (10%)**
   - Every hard inquiry can drop your score a few points temporarily. Apply for new cards strategically.
5. **Credit Mix (10%)**
   - A mix of credit types (credit cards, loans, auto financing, etc.) shows you can manage different forms of debt responsibly.

Pro Tip: Focus most on **payment history** and **utilization**—together, they make up 65% of your score.

Step 2: Use Credit Cards to Build Positive Credit Habits

Every time you use a card and pay it off responsibly, you're reinforcing a strong credit profile. Here's how to build habits that boost your score while hacking rewards:

- **Pay your balance weekly** (not just monthly). This keeps your utilization low and prevents forgotten bills.
- **Keep utilization under 10%** of each card's limit—even if you plan to pay in full later.
- **Don't close old accounts** unless the fee outweighs the benefit.
- **Open new cards only when needed**, and space them out every 3–6 months.

Example: If you have a $10,000 credit limit across all cards, try to keep your total balance **under $1,000 at all times**.

Step 3: Increase Your Credit Limit Without Increasing Your Spending

One of the fastest ways to improve your score is to **increase your credit limit** while keeping your spending the same. This lowers your credit utilization ratio.

You can do this by:

- Requesting a credit limit increase from your card issuer (usually available in the app or online)

- Getting approved for a new card with a high limit
- Allowing automatic increases (some banks offer this every 6–12 months if you pay on time)

Important: Do **not** see a higher limit as permission to spend more. Treat it like a safety net that boosts your score.

Step 4: Monitor Your Credit and Dispute Errors

Just like you check your bank account or budget, you should **monitor your credit report** regularly. Mistakes happen, and they can hurt your score if left unchecked.

Here's what to do:

- Use **AnnualCreditReport.com** to get your free reports from Experian, TransUnion, and Equifax once a year.
- Use free credit monitoring apps like **Credit Karma**, **Credit Sesame**, or **Experian** to stay on top of changes.
- Look for:
    - Late payments reported in error
    - Accounts you don't recognize

- Incorrect balances
- Accounts not updated after payoff

If you find an error:

- File a dispute online through the credit bureau's website.
- Provide documentation (e.g., payment confirmations).
- The bureau has 30–45 days to respond.

Step 5: Avoid the Most Common Credit Card Mistakes

To build credit while hacking rewards, you must avoid these common traps:

1. **Carrying a balance to "build credit"**
    - **MYTH.** You do NOT need to carry a balance or pay interest to build credit. Just use the card and pay it off in full.
2. **Applying for too many cards too quickly**
    - Space out your applications. Too many inquiries in a short time can lower your score and scare lenders.

3. **Using over 30% of your credit limit**
    - Even temporarily. Utilization is often calculated based on **statement balances**, so keep them low before the statement closes.
4. **Ignoring due dates**
    - Set **autopay** for the full amount due. Late payments hurt more than almost any other factor.
5. **Closing old cards without checking the impact**
    - If it's your oldest account or a card with a high limit, consider **downgrading** it instead of closing.

Step 6: Build Toward Your Long-Term Credit Goals

Credit hacking isn't just about points—it's about positioning yourself for **bigger opportunities**:

- Qualifying for **low mortgage rates**
- Getting **higher credit limits**
- Accessing **premium travel and business credit cards**

- Being approved for **business loans or HELOCs**

Set these goals:

- Credit score target: 750+
- Credit limit goal: $50,000+ total available
- Length of credit: Maintain accounts for 7+ years
- Payment history: 100% on-time

Chapter Summary and Action Plan

1. **Know your FICO score factors**, and focus on payment history and utilization.
2. **Use your cards like a credit-building tool**—low balances, on-time payments, and strategic spending.
3. **Increase your limits gradually**, and treat them as leverage, not temptation.
4. **Monitor your credit reports regularly**, and dispute any errors immediately.
5. **Avoid common traps** like carrying a balance or closing old cards.

6. **Think long-term**—your future borrowing power is shaped by the habits you start today.

When done right, building credit while hacking rewards becomes a win-win. You enjoy the perks now—and open doors to bigger opportunities later.

The Story of Janelle's Credit Comeback

Janelle Thompson stared at the email on her laptop screen. It was another denial.

She had applied for a mid-tier travel rewards card—a basic one, nothing flashy—and yet again, the message was the same: *"We regret to inform you..."* She sighed, closed the tab, and pushed her coffee aside. It wasn't just about the card. It was about what the denial represented.

Janelle had been through a rough stretch. A messy divorce, job loss during the pandemic, and a medical emergency had thrown her finances into chaos. She hadn't filed for bankruptcy, but her credit score had plummeted into the low 600s. She was rebuilding now—steady job, stable income—but her credit history told a story she was no longer living.

She'd recently discovered credit card hacking and was fascinated. Free flights? Cashback? Hotel upgrades? It sounded like a dream. But as she dug deeper, she realized something crucial: **before she could play the game, she had to repair the board.**

So she made a decision. No more impulse applications. No more guessing games. She would **rebuild her credit strategically**—and do it while laying the groundwork for future rewards.

Step one: she pulled her credit reports from all three bureaus using AnnualCreditReport.com. It was overwhelming at first. Old accounts, a couple of late payments, and some credit cards she hadn't used in years. But she took notes.

She opened a spreadsheet and listed everything:

- Open accounts
- Payment histories
- Utilization rates
- Derogatory marks

It wasn't pretty—but it was honest.

Step two: she set up **autopay** for every bill she had—utilities, insurance, and her remaining credit card. She made a rule: **every Friday was "Money Check-In Day."** She'd review her balances, update her spreadsheet, and make early payments. It became a habit. Like brushing her teeth. It gave her control.

Then she found out about **secured credit cards**. She applied for one with a $300 deposit and was approved. It was a small step—but for her, it was huge. She used it for gas and groceries only. Never more than $100 at a time. Paid it off **twice a month**.

After four months, her score ticked up—632 to 658.

Then she called her bank and requested a **credit limit increase** on her older card. She had paid on time for over a year. To her surprise, they doubled her limit.

Her utilization dropped. Her score went up again.

She was building.

Janelle also signed up for **Experian Boost**, adding her phone and utility payments to her credit file. It gave her a 15-point jump overnight. Not magic—just momentum.

Six months in, she was back in the 700s. For the first time in years, she smiled when she checked her credit score.

Then came the moment she'd been waiting for: she applied for a **real rewards card**—the Amex Blue Cash Everyday. No annual fee, decent cashback, and a modest welcome bonus. She was approved. Limit: $2,000.

She used it only for groceries and streaming subscriptions. Set autopay. Never carried a balance. After three months, she'd earned $78 in cashback—and another credit limit increase.

By the end of the year, Janelle had:

- Three open cards
- Over $6,000 in total credit
- 100% on-time payments
- Utilization under 8%
- A credit score of 742

But more than numbers, she had confidence. She no longer feared credit. She understood it. She used it intentionally—not just to earn rewards, but to secure her future.

She started mentoring her younger cousin who was just getting started with credit. Taught her how to track spending, check reports, avoid minimum payments, and keep balances low. She told her:

> "Credit isn't the problem. How we use it is."

Janelle booked her first reward flight to Chicago that fall—paid entirely with cashback. As she boarded the plane, she thought about the journey. Not the flight. The **real** journey.

From denied... to approved. From stressed... to empowered. From buried in credit fear... to building credit freedom.

And she knew this was just the beginning.

Chapter 7: How to Travel for Free Using Points and Miles

One of the biggest motivators for credit card hackers is the dream of **traveling for free**—flights, hotels, rental cars, upgrades, even luxury experiences. What sounds like a fantasy is actually possible when you learn how to **accumulate and redeem points and miles effectively**.

In this chapter, you'll learn the core strategy behind booking **free or deeply discounted travel**, and how to plan trips using your rewards like a pro.

Step 1: Choose a Flexible Travel Rewards Ecosystem

Not all points are created equal. To travel for free consistently, focus on cards that earn **flexible points** that can transfer to multiple airlines or hotel partners.

Top ecosystems include:

- **Chase Ultimate Rewards**
    - Transfer partners: United, Hyatt, Southwest, British Airways, etc.
    - Cards: Chase Sapphire Preferred, Sapphire Reserve, Ink Business Preferred

- **American Express Membership Rewards**
  - Transfer partners: Delta, Air Canada, Hilton, ANA, etc.
  - Cards: Amex Gold, Amex Platinum, Amex Business Platinum
- **Citi ThankYou Points**
  - Transfer partners: Turkish Airlines, Avianca, Choice Hotels, etc.
  - Cards: Citi Premier, Citi Rewards+
- **Capital One Miles**
  - Transfer partners: Air France/KLM, Emirates, Wyndham, etc.
  - Cards: Capital One Venture, Venture X

Why it matters: Flexibility gives you the best chance to find **award availability** and **maximize point value**, especially when booking international or peak-season travel.

Step 2: Understand the Booking Value of Your Points

Before booking anything, understand how much value you're getting for your points. You want to aim for **at least 1.5 cents**

per point, and ideally **2+ cents** with travel redemptions.

Example:

- A flight costs $500.
- It requires 25,000 points.
- $500 ÷ 25,000 = **2 cents per point (cpp)** – that's excellent value.

Use calculators on sites like:

- The Points Guy (TPG)
- AwardWallet
- NerdWallet

If the value is below **1 cent per point**, consider paying with cash and saving your points for a better redemption.

Step 3: Transfer Points to Airline or Hotel Partners

Transferring your points from your credit card account to a travel partner can **more than double their value**. But it takes planning.

Here's how to do it:

1. Search for availability directly on the airline or hotel

website (not your credit card's portal).

2. Create a loyalty account with that airline or hotel.
3. Log in to your credit card rewards dashboard.
4. Select "Transfer Points" and choose the partner.
5. Enter your loyalty account info and the number of points.
6. Confirm the transfer (note: most transfers are **one-way and non-reversible**).

Pro Tip: Always confirm the seat or room is available **before** transferring.

Step 4: Know the Sweet Spots and Award Charts

Sweet spots are redemptions where the value of your points is disproportionately high.

Here are examples:

- **Hyatt Hotels via Chase Ultimate Rewards**
    - Park Hyatt NYC: $1,200/night or 30,000 points = **4 cpp**
- **ANA Roundtrip Business Class via Amex**

    - U.S. to Japan for 75,000 points roundtrip

- **Turkish Airlines via Citi ThankYou Points**
    - U.S. to Hawaii roundtrip for 15,000 points in economy

- **British Airways Avios**
    - Short-haul flights in the U.S. (under 650 miles) for 7,500 points + $5.60

Always check for **low surcharges** and **partner availability**, as some programs have better deals for specific routes.

Step 5: Use Travel Portals When Simplicity Matters

If you don't want to transfer points or deal with loyalty programs, use your card's **travel portal** to book directly. Some portals even **boost the value** of your points.

Examples:

- Chase Sapphire Preferred: Points worth **1.25x**
- Chase Sapphire Reserve: Points worth **1.5x**
- Amex Travel: Sometimes offers exclusive rates and upgrades

This is a great option when:

- You want to book a flight on a low-cost carrier (like JetBlue or Spirit)
- You're booking a hotel that's not part of a major chain
- You don't want to worry about blackout dates or reward availability

Downside: You may not earn frequent flyer miles or elite status benefits.

Step 6: Maximize Hotel Stays Using Points

Hotel rewards can be just as valuable—if not more—than flights. With hotel points, you can often stay multiple nights for free, especially at mid-tier properties.

Top hotel programs include:

- **Hyatt** (via Chase)
- **Hilton Honors** (via Amex)
- **Marriott Bonvoy** (via Chase or Amex)
- **Choice Privileges** (via Citi)

Tips to Maximize Hotel Points:

- Look for **5th night free** promos (Hilton and Marriott)
- Use your co-branded hotel card for **free anniversary nights**
- Avoid luxury properties with inflated point requirements—focus on mid-tier hotels in great locations
- Book early for peak travel seasons

Chapter Summary and Action Plan

1. Focus on cards that earn **flexible points** for maximum travel value.
2. Always calculate your **cents-per-point value** before redeeming.
3. **Transfer points to travel partners** when you want to maximize value—but plan carefully.
4. Learn your program's **sweet spots** and use award charts when available.
5. Use **travel portals** for simplicity or when partner options don't fit.
6. Don't forget to **redeem points for hotel stays,**

where long stays and fifth-night-free perks can stretch your value.

Travel hacking isn't just for jetsetters—it's for everyday people who spend smart, plan ahead, and use the right cards at the right time. With a few smart moves, you can start traveling better, more often—and sometimes, for free.

The Story of Luis's First-Class Surprise

Luis Rivera wasn't rich, but you wouldn't have guessed that from the way he strolled through the business class lounge at JFK, sipping ginger tea and staring out the window at the massive Airbus A350 that would soon carry him across the Atlantic.

In a few hours, he'd be in Paris—his first trip to Europe—and he'd paid less than $100 for the entire journey.

Only six months earlier, Luis had never heard the term "travel hacking." He worked as an elementary school teacher in Miami and had just finished paying off the last of his credit card debt from his twenties. Travel was always a dream, but one that felt just out of reach. Flights were expensive. Hotels even more so. He had never flown outside the U.S., let alone sat anywhere near the front of the plane.

It all changed when his friend Jamie invited him to a backyard barbecue and casually mentioned she had just booked a trip to Rome using credit card points.

Luis was floored. "Wait, like... you didn't pay anything?"

"Well," Jamie laughed, "I paid $52 in taxes, but yeah. First class. Entire thing booked with Amex points."

That night, Luis went home and typed *"how to fly for free using credit cards"* into YouTube. Three hours later, he had a notebook full of scribbles and a new obsession.

He started by applying for the **Chase Sapphire Preferred**, following the advice of every travel blog he could find. The sign-up bonus at the time was 60,000 points after spending $4,000 in three months. Luis knew he'd have to be smart–he didn't spend much–but he found ways to make it work. He used the card to pay his rent through a portal with a 1% fee, bought grocery store gift cards for gas and everyday purchases, and paid for his friend's wedding venue deposit (she reimbursed him right away).

He hit the bonus just in time.

With his points in hand, Luis did something different–he planned **backwards**. He didn't pick a destination and hope his points worked. He searched for **award availability** first.

That's when he found it: a one-way business class ticket from New York to Paris on Air France. Retail price? $3,400. Points cost? 55,000 Chase points transferred to Flying Blue, plus $87 in taxes.

He transferred the points. Waited anxiously. And when the confirmation email came through, he sat back and smiled. He had done it.

Then came the hotel. Luis used the rest of his points to book three nights at a boutique Hyatt in the heart of the Marais district—22,000 points per night. If he'd paid cash, it would have been nearly $1,200.

The night before his flight, he could barely sleep. He kept checking the app, making sure the booking hadn't vanished. He packed carefully—passport, chargers, one pair of clean sneakers, and a notebook to journal the entire experience.

At the airport, he checked in at the Sky Priority counter. No line. No rush. He breezed through security and entered the Air France lounge, where soft jazz played and the espresso machine hissed in the background.

Sitting in a lounge chair, Luis looked around and chuckled. "I teach third grade," he thought. "How am I here?"

The answer, he knew, wasn't luck. It was knowledge. It was

strategy. It was points.

The flight itself was everything he imagined. A lie-flat seat, a three-course meal, champagne at takeoff. He watched a French film, took a nap, and woke up just as they descended into Charles de Gaulle airport.

He took the train into the city. Walked along the Seine. Ate crepes from a street vendor and listened to street musicians play under golden streetlights.

The best part? Every time someone asked how much he paid for the trip, he just smiled.

Luis spent the next few days wandering museums and bookstores, journaling the entire journey. At night, he returned to his hotel, knowing it was all booked with points.

After he got home, he started planning his next trip—to Japan. He had already opened an Amex Gold card and started earning points for takeout and groceries.

For Luis, travel was no longer a dream. It was a system. A way of life. And it all started with a single card, a sign-up bonus, and a decision to stop saying, "I can't afford that."

Now, whenever someone asked him how he pulled it off, he didn't just give them tips—he handed them a pen and said,

Chapter 8: Advanced Strategies for Maximizing Every Dollar

Once you've built a strong foundation—earning points, redeeming for value, managing multiple cards, and building credit—what's next? This chapter dives into **advanced-level tactics** used by experienced credit card hackers to **amplify rewards**, **stretch redemptions**, and **turn everyday spending into extraordinary value.**

If you want to unlock elite travel, thousands in annual cashback, or even build a side income from your rewards system, these strategies are for you.

Step 1: Leverage Multipliers with Stackable Offers

The smartest hackers don't just earn 1–5% on purchases—they **stack offers** to earn 10% or more from the same transaction.

Here's how:

1. **Card Category Bonus** – Use a card that gives elevated points for the purchase type (e.g., 4x at restaurants).

2. **Shopping Portal Bonus** – Use sites like **Rakuten**, **TopCashback**, or **Chase/Amex shopping portals** for additional 1%–10%.

3. **Targeted Card Offers** – Activate targeted promotions (e.g., "Spend $50 at Best Buy, get $10 back").

4. **Coupon & Deal Extensions** – Tools like **Honey** or **Capital One Shopping** add auto-discounts and rebates.

Example: You buy $200 worth of shoes at Nike.com:

- Use a card that earns 3x on online purchases = 600 points
- Go through Rakuten portal for 10% cashback = $20
- Use an Amex Offer for $10 back on $100 spend
- Apply a 15% discount code via a browser extension

Total Value Earned: Over $50 in cashback and points

Stacking offers is **compound hacking**—a key trait of advanced users.

Step 2: Time Your Large Purchases for Maximum Bonus Returns

Big purchases—appliances, electronics, travel bookings, even taxes—can be timed to trigger massive value if aligned with:

- **Welcome bonuses** (e.g., spend $4,000 in 3 months)
- **Quarterly category activations** (e.g., 5% back on travel Q3)
- **New card spend thresholds** (e.g., spend $15,000 in a year for bonus points)

Advanced Tip: If you know you'll be spending a large sum (wedding, renovations, medical bills), **plan ahead and open a card 30–60 days before the expense.**

Then:

- Use the purchase to hit the bonus
- Stack it with shopping portals and offers
- Redeem the bonus for a high-value trip or cashback

This method turns a one-time expense into a long-term reward.

Step 3: Use Multiple Cards as a Unified Ecosystem

Most beginners use cards in isolation. Advanced hackers treat their cards as a **team**.

The Ecosystem Strategy:

- Use **category cards** for their strengths (e.g., 5% on groceries, 3x on gas)
- Funnel those rewards into a **premium card** with a stronger redemption portal (e.g., Chase Freedom points transferred to Chase Sapphire Reserve)
- Combine **personal and business cards** to amplify points and keep categories separated

Example Setup:

- Chase Freedom Flex (5% rotating)
- Chase Ink Business Cash (5% on office supplies, internet)
- Chase Sapphire Preferred (hub card for travel redemption)

Result: You earn points at 3x–5x across multiple spend types, then redeem through one card's portal for **25–50% more value.**

Step 4: Optimize Authorized Users and Household Rewards

If you live with a spouse, partner, roommate, or family member, you can **maximize rewards as a unit.**

Options include:

- **Add authorized users** to cards to hit minimum spend faster and earn referral bonuses
- **Refer family members** to cards you already have (most issuers give $50–$200 per referral)
- **Pool points** from Chase, Amex, or Citi for a major travel redemption
- **Split spend across cards strategically** (e.g., one uses the 5% dining card, the other uses the 6% grocery card)

Pro Tip: Some cards (like Amex Platinum) offer **elite status** to both the primary and authorized users—great for hotel upgrades and lounge access.

Step 5: Use Rewards as Capital to Build Other Income Streams

Advanced credit card hackers often use rewards to:

- Travel to attend business conferences (points pay for flights and hotels)
- Use cashback to fund investments, courses, or business tools
- Open **business credit cards** and funnel their side hustle expenses to build even more points

Case Example: A freelancer opens the Amex Blue Business Plus (2x on all purchases). He uses it to pay for:

- Advertising
- Software
- Client gifts

He earns over 100,000 Membership Rewards in a year—worth $1,000–$2,000 in travel or more when transferred to partners.

That's **leveraged value**—earning while spending, then reinvesting rewards into business growth or personal freedom.

Chapter Summary and Action Plan

1. **Stack every purchase** using bonus categories, portals, and offers.
2. **Plan large purchases** around welcome bonuses or category promotions.
3. **Build a multi-card system** where rewards are pooled into one high-value portal.
4. **Coordinate with family** or partners to multiply earning potential.
5. **Think like an investor**—use rewards to support business, growth, or income-generating opportunities.

Advanced credit card hacking is about more than free flights—it's a mindset of **intelligent optimization**, turning every dollar you spend into a smarter version of itself. You don't need more money—you need to be more strategic with what you already spend.

The Story of Nia's Everyday Empire

Nia Jefferson wasn't flashy. She didn't post credit card selfies or humblebrag about lounge access on social media. She was a 39-year-old single mom from Charlotte, North Carolina, with two kids, a full-time job, and a growing photography side hustle. What set Nia apart wasn't how much she earned—it was **how strategically she spent.**

To most people, she looked like any busy professional. But to those who knew her system, Nia was a credit card hacker with **elite-level precision.**

Her journey started with a simple cashback card years ago, but once she paid off her debt and built her credit to a 760, she began to study how points and miles could change her financial trajectory—not just for travel, but for leverage.

Her first breakthrough came when she opened the **Chase Ink Business Cash** for her photography side gig. The welcome bonus was 75,000 points after $6,000 in three months. Nia timed it perfectly. She had a wedding shoot coming up and needed new lenses, lighting gear, and a second camera body. She bought everything with the new card—and hit the bonus in less than six weeks.

Next, she opened the **Amex Gold** and used it for groceries and dining, which accounted for nearly $1,200 a month between her family and client meals. That gave her 4x points on nearly $15,000 annually—**60,000 Amex points** on autopilot.

But Nia didn't stop there.

She started **stacking offers**. Before buying anything online—whether it was kids' school shoes, client albums, or holiday gifts—she checked shopping portals. She bookmarked **Rakuten**, **Chase Offers**, and **TopCashback**, and installed browser extensions that alerted her to cash bonuses. Every purchase became a puzzle. Which card? Which portal? Which offer?

Then came the strategy that changed everything: **planned purchases.**

In February, she knew she'd be paying $2,000 in business insurance, annual software subscriptions, and tax prep fees. So in January, she applied for a **Citi Premier** card, offering 60,000 ThankYou Points after $4,000 in 3 months. She stacked the expenses, bought gift cards for future travel, and even paid her CPA through a low-fee payment portal to hit the bonus fast.

By April, she had enough points to cover a family trip to California—flights and hotels included.

But her proudest hack wasn't a free flight.

It was the **cycle she'd created**.

Every major bill or expense became an opportunity to:

- Earn a welcome bonus
- Stack category points
- Leverage rewards into travel, cashback, or business investments

She tracked everything in a color-coded spreadsheet:

- Card name, limit, bonus timeline
- Category strengths
- Current offers
- Statement due dates
- Redemption goals

Her Amex Gold had a sticky note: “Groceries + Dining Only.” Her Sapphire card said: “Use for Travel Portal.” Her Citi card? “Gift cards + Gas.” Even her kids got involved. They would ask, “Which card do we use for Target this week?”

Over time, she layered in **authorized users**—adding her sister and her teen son, who was learning about credit. Every purchase they made was intentional and tracked. She earned referral bonuses for helping her best friend and sister get cards. One month, she earned **$500 in referral bonuses alone.**

Nia wasn't just hacking points. She was **building an everyday empire.**

The turning point came when her son, 17 at the time, asked how to earn points for his graduation trip to New York. She smiled and handed him a notebook.

"We'll build your first travel plan together," she said. "But you have to understand the system."

That night, they built a mock card ecosystem: one for groceries, one for gas, one for school expenses. They used real calculators, reward portals, and even printed boarding passes from mock redemptions.

Her son looked up, wide-eyed. "We can fly for free? Just from buying what we already buy?"

Nia nodded. "We don't spend more. We just spend smarter."

By the end of the year, Nia had earned:

- Over 350,000 total points across 4 programs
- $1,200 in cashback

- Two round-trip flights to Europe
- Four nights at a Hyatt in San Francisco
- And a new camera lens—paid entirely with points

But more than that, she had created something bigger: **financial freedom through intention.**

Every dollar had a job. Every purchase had a purpose.

And she didn't just hack credit cards—she taught others how to **leverage the life they already live** into one filled with options, opportunity, and adventure.

Chapter 9: Avoiding the Pitfalls of Credit Card Hacking

Credit card hacking can unlock thousands of dollars in free travel, cashback, and perks—but without careful management, it can also lead to overspending, debt, stress, and even a lower credit score. In this chapter, you'll learn the most common **mistakes to avoid**, how to recognize the **warning signs** of misuse, and how to **course-correct quickly** if things get out of control.

Advanced strategies are powerful—but only if you're protecting your financial foundation.

Step 1: Never Carry a Balance to Earn Rewards

One of the most damaging myths in credit is the idea that you should carry a balance to build your credit score or earn more rewards. This is **completely false**.

- You earn **rewards based on what you spend**, not on what you carry as a balance.
- Carrying a balance means you're paying **interest**, often at 18%–29%, which **erases any benefit** of your points or cashback.

Rule: Always pay off your statement balance in full. Set up **autopay** to prevent missing payments. If you can't afford to pay off a purchase by the end of the billing cycle, you shouldn't put it on the card.

Step 2: Don't Chase Bonuses Without a Plan

Welcome bonuses are one of the most exciting parts of credit card hacking—but chasing too many at once can backfire.

Here's what can go wrong:

- You miss a **minimum spend requirement**, losing the bonus and racking up unnecessary debt.
- You open too many cards in a short period, triggering a drop in your credit score due to multiple hard inquiries.
- You lose track of payment due dates, leading to late fees or missed payments.

Best Practices:

- Space out applications every **90–120 days**.
- Map out the spend you already expect before applying.
- Set a calendar reminder for the spend deadline and track your progress weekly.

Step 3: Watch Your Credit Utilization Like a Hawk

Even if you pay in full each month, your **credit utilization** can still hurt your score if you let your balances report too high on statement day.

Example:

- Credit limit: $5,000
- You spend: $3,000
- Utilization: 60%
- Even if paid off, this may hurt your score temporarily

Fixes:

- Make **mid-cycle payments** to lower your balance before the statement closes.
- Spread expenses across multiple cards to avoid high individual utilization.
- Ask for **credit limit increases** every 6–12 months to expand your cushion.

Goal: Keep overall utilization under 30%, and preferably under 10% for optimal scores.

Step 4: Don't Let Annual Fees Eat Your Rewards

Some premium cards come with high annual fees—sometimes $95, $250, or even $695. These can be **worth it** if you use the benefits... but many people forget and end up **losing money**.

What to watch for:

- Did you use all included credits (e.g., dining, Uber, travel, hotel night)?
- Are you getting more value in points than the fee costs?
- Are you holding a premium card **just because it looks good?**

Action Step: Every year, set a reminder 11 months after opening a card. Review your usage:

- If the value exceeds the fee, keep it.
- If not, **downgrade to a no-fee version** or cancel after redeeming your points.

Step 5: Avoid Account Clutter and Mental Overload

The average credit hacker manages 5–10 cards. That's doable—if you're organized. But adding cards without a system leads to:

- Missed payments
- Overlapping benefits
- Underutilized perks
- Decision fatigue

Solutions:

- Use a **credit card tracker** (spreadsheet or app like MaxRewards or Travel Freely)
- Rotate cards seasonally based on bonus categories
- Carry only 2–3 cards in your physical wallet—keep the rest for online or targeted spend
- Use calendar alerts for **renewal dates**, **credit anniversaries**, and **quarterly activations**

Step 6: Don't Let Credit Cards Replace a Budget

This is where many high earners fail: they assume rewards are a substitute for discipline. But the core rule remains—**spend only what you can afford**.

Make your cards work inside a real budget:

- Use a budgeting app like **YNAB**, **EveryDollar**, or **Mint** to track spending
- Set category limits—even on credit cards
- Check your rewards weekly and match them to your goals

Using cards without a budget is like flying a plane without instruments—you might stay in the air, but you're headed for turbulence.

Chapter Summary and Action Plan

1. **Never carry a balance** just to earn points—interest wipes out rewards.
2. **Don't chase cards too quickly**—strategize applications and spend wisely.
3. **Track your utilization** and avoid letting high balances report to the credit bureaus.
4. **Annual fees must be justified**—review benefits every 11 months.
5. **Keep your cards organized**—too many without a system will cause mistakes.

6. **Always spend within a budget**—your points should be a byproduct of control, not a replacement for it.

Hacking credit cards successfully isn't just about earning more—it's about protecting what you've built. Every reward should be a **bonus**, not a burden.

The Story of Tyler's Reset

Tyler Grant didn't start credit card hacking with bad intentions. Quite the opposite. He had read the blogs, watched the YouTube tutorials, and even downloaded a few apps to track his points. He'd opened his first travel rewards card just after landing his first remote marketing job. "Might as well get paid to live my life," he told himself.

And at first, everything went smoothly. He hit the sign-up bonus. He booked a free hotel stay. He transferred points to an airline and flew to visit friends in Chicago for just $28 in taxes. He was hooked.

But then... he got greedy.

One morning, he saw an email with the subject line: "Earn 80,000 Points—Limited Time Offer." It was a premium card with a $695 annual fee. He applied. Approved. Then another card caught his eye: 5% cashback on groceries and gas. "Makes sense," he thought. "I'll use that too."

Then came another. And another.

Within eight months, Tyler had **seven open cards**, five with annual fees, and three different points programs to manage. He had set up a spreadsheet—once. But it hadn't been updated in months. He had calendar reminders, but some were buried under work emails and ignored.

Then the due dates started to pile up.

Tyler forgot to pay one of his cards—just by a few days. He'd been traveling, didn't see the statement, and missed the payment. He paid it off right away, but the late fee hit—and worse, his credit score dropped 46 points.

That stung.

Next, he noticed his total balances creeping higher. He had promised himself he'd pay everything off in full, but somehow, he had racked up over $4,200 across his cards. Mostly small things: takeout, Amazon orders, Uber rides, a few impulse buys. It didn't feel like much when he swiped. But when the statements arrived, it hit hard.

He started only paying minimums. Then he stopped opening the statements.

The tipping point came when he tried to book a flight to Costa Rica using his points. He logged into the airline portal and... his balance was gone.

Confused, he called the issuer.

"Your account was closed due to inactivity and annual fee non-payment," the agent said. "Unfortunately, your points expired when the account closed."

That night, Tyler sat on his couch with his laptop, his credit report, and a pit in his stomach.

He had tried to hack the system... but the system had quietly taken control of him.

He was embarrassed—but determined not to let the story end there.

So he did what he should have done months ago.

He made a list of all his cards—balances, due dates, rewards types, annual fees. He created a new spreadsheet. Then he set **autopay** for every account.

Next, he transferred balances from his high-interest cards to a 0% APR card he still had open. He made a 6-month payoff plan.

He called the issuers of the cards he wasn't using and **downgraded** most of them to no-fee versions. He kept only three active cards: one for dining and groceries, one for travel, and one flat-rate cashback card.

He created a "Money Check-In" every Sunday night—30 minutes with his budget and his credit card tracker. He paid his cards **before** the statements closed to lower his reported utilization.

And the late payment? He wrote a goodwill letter and submitted it to the issuer. Two weeks later, the late mark was removed. His score rebounded.

In five months, Tyler:

- Paid off 80% of his balances
- Reclaimed his 740+ credit score
- Earned two small sign-up bonuses by planning spend strategically
- Booked a flight using points—**and actually got on the plane this time**

Sitting on that flight, journal in hand, Tyler wrote a note to himself:

> "This is how you do it. Controlled, clean, intentional. Never again will I let points be the reason I lose money."

He wasn't a beginner anymore. He'd fallen into the trap—and climbed out. Stronger. Smarter. More focused.

From that day on, Tyler didn't chase points. He **earned them**—on his terms.

Chapter 10: Building a Long-Term Credit Card Hacking Strategy

You've learned how to earn points, redeem them, manage multiple cards, and avoid common mistakes—but the real magic happens when you **build a long-term system** that runs on autopilot. A smart credit card hacking strategy isn't about chasing every bonus or opening the flashiest card—it's about creating a **repeatable, organized process** that works year after year.

In this chapter, you'll learn how to build a strategy that grows with you, protects your credit, and continues to generate free travel, cashback, and financial flexibility well into the future.

Step 1: Define Your Long-Term Goals

Before you add another card or redeem another point, define your "why." This keeps you focused and prevents distractions.

Ask yourself:

- Do I want to travel more? If so, where and how often?
- Do I want to earn passive cashback on regular expenses?

- Do I want to build credit for home or business financing?
- Do I want to use rewards to support my business or side hustle?

Your answers determine your card choices, redemption strategies, and spending patterns.

Examples:

- If you want to travel once per year to Europe: focus on points that transfer to international airline partners like Air France, ANA, or Turkish Airlines.
- If your priority is cash back for everyday savings: focus on 2% flat-rate cards and rotating bonus categories.

Step 2: Choose and Maintain a Core "Rewards Ecosystem"

Pick one or two rewards programs that match your goals, and build your strategy around them.

Top Ecosystems:

- **Chase Ultimate Rewards** – Best for beginners; flexible transfers to airlines and hotels; strong portal value.

- **Amex Membership Rewards** – Premium travel perks, high value for advanced users, lots of transfer partners.
- **Citi ThankYou Points** – Great for international travel; less intuitive but valuable for certain redemptions.
- **Capital One Miles** – Simple system with strong travel partners and decent redemption rates.

How to maintain your ecosystem:

- Pair a **core card** (like Sapphire Preferred or Amex Gold) with **category-specific or no-fee cards** to maximize earnings.
- Pool all points into your "hub" card to simplify redemptions.
- Review your point balances and upcoming trips quarterly.

Step 3: Create an Annual Card Review Schedule

Set a reminder every year—ideally one month before each card's annual fee is due—to review your card portfolio.

Checklist:

- Am I using the benefits of this card (credits, perks, insurance)?
- Did I earn enough rewards to justify the fee?
- Are better offers available from competitors?
- Can I **downgrade** or **product change** this card to a no-fee version?

This keeps your wallet lean and your strategy intentional. Don't hold onto cards just because you've had them a long time—unless they're helping your credit age or limit.

Step 4: Rotate New Cards Strategically

Add 1–3 new cards per year, spaced at least **90–120 days apart**. Each card should serve one of three purposes:

1. Earn a **new welcome bonus**
2. Cover a **category you're not currently maximizing**
3. Replace or upgrade an underperforming card

Advanced Tip: Align new card openings with planned expenses—like vacations, holidays, tax season, or business purchases—to meet minimum spend effortlessly.

Create a card planning calendar with:

- Application month
- Welcome bonus requirement
- Spend deadline
- Redemption goal

This reduces overwhelm and helps you maintain a sustainable pace.

Step 5: Build Redemption Plans in Advance

Don't wait until you're ready to travel to figure out how to use your points. Have 1–2 **target redemptions** in mind and reverse-engineer your card choices around them.

Example Goals:

- Book 2 roundtrip flights to Italy next summer using Chase points
- Stay 5 nights in a Hyatt hotel in Hawaii using a free night certificate + points
- Redeem $500 in cashback for end-of-year holiday expenses

Having a specific plan means:

- You'll avoid wasting points on low-value redemptions
- You can time redemptions during point transfer bonuses or award sales
- You can leverage cards with benefits that match your goals (e.g., travel insurance, elite status, transfer perks)

Step 6: Automate, Track, and Reinvest Your Rewards

Once your system is in place, **automate** as much as possible:

- Use autopay for all cards (full balance)
- Set up monthly reminders to check balances and reward balances
- Use spreadsheets or tools like **MaxRewards**, **AwardWallet**, or **Travel Freely** to track rewards and expiry dates

Then, use your rewards **intentionally**:

- Fund travel that aligns with your personal or business goals
- Use cashback to invest in courses, tools, or your side hustle

- Reinvest your value—don't let it sit unused

The smartest hackers don't just earn—they **redeem with purpose** and create systems that run themselves.

Chapter Summary and Long-Term Strategy Plan

1. **Start with your "why"**—define your travel, savings, or freedom goals.
2. **Choose a rewards ecosystem** that aligns with your lifestyle.
3. **Review your cards annually** and downgrade or cancel strategically.
4. **Apply for new cards intentionally**, aligned with planned spend.
5. **Plan redemptions in advance** so points go toward high-value experiences.
6. **Automate and track everything** to minimize stress and maximize value.

Credit card hacking isn't just a short-term game—it's a lifestyle upgrade. With a long-term plan in place, you'll enjoy **years of free travel, savings, and financial empowerment**—all by being intentional with the money you already spend.

Final Chapter: Living the Credit Card Hacker's Lifestyle

By now, you've learned how to master every major element of credit card hacking—from choosing the right cards and earning rewards to managing multiple accounts, avoiding debt traps, and building long-term strategies.

But the most important takeaway isn't the free flights, cashback, or lounge access—it's the mindset you've developed. A **credit card hacker's lifestyle** isn't about chasing perks—it's about controlling your financial choices, using systems to create freedom, and making your money work smarter, not harder.

This final chapter will help you lock in the habits, systems, and mindset that transform this strategy from a fun experiment into a **sustainable way of life.**

Step 1: See Credit as a Tool—Not a Crutch

Credit is not evil. It's not dangerous. It's not something to fear.

Used properly, it's one of the most powerful tools in your financial toolkit. But just like any tool, it must be handled with care, intention, and structure.

A credit card hacker:

- Spends only what they can afford
- Uses credit to **earn**, not to **escape**
- Treats points and cashback as a **bonus**, not a bailout
- Makes decisions based on **value**, not emotion

Your score, your limits, and your rewards are reflections of your behavior—not your identity. Own them. Direct them. Improve them.

Step 2: Make Smart Money Moves Automatic

The real key to success is consistency—and the best way to stay consistent is to **remove friction**.

Smart hackers automate:

- **Full-balance autopay** for every card
- **Monthly card check-ins** using calendar reminders
- **Quarterly ecosystem reviews** to spot gaps and opportunities
- **Goal-based redemptions**, so points are spent on things that matter

You shouldn't have to rely on memory or motivation. Your system should support you—quietly, efficiently, and every month.

Step 3: Use Points to Expand Your World

Points are more than currency—they're **permission**.

They give you permission to:

- Travel more
- See family more often
- Take a break without guilt
- Attend that conference you couldn't afford before
- Stay in places that were once "out of reach"

Credit card hackers don't hoard points—they **spend them wisely** on things that align with their purpose.

Use your rewards to invest in **yourself**, your **business**, your **family**, or your **freedom**. The value isn't just in the dollar amount—it's in what that dollar lets you do.

Step 4: Teach Others What You Know

You now have knowledge that most people never learn. The majority of credit card users either:

- Avoid credit entirely out of fear
- Abuse it out of desperation
- Or ignore the rewards they're entitled to

But not you.

Now that you've mastered this strategy, share it. Teach a family member how to build their credit. Help a friend earn their first free trip. Show your kids how to use credit responsibly from day one.

When you empower others, your wins multiply.

Step 5: Keep Learning and Evolving

Credit card programs change. Reward structures shift. New opportunities arise. Your life will evolve too—new goals, new expenses, new possibilities.

The best credit card hackers are lifelong learners.

Stay up to date with:

- Travel rewards blogs like The Points Guy, Doctor of Credit, and One Mile at a Time
- YouTube channels and podcasts that share current strategies
- Community forums and groups (Reddit's r/churning is a great example)

Every few months, ask yourself:

- What changed in my spending?
- Are there new bonuses I can earn?
- Can I get more value from the cards I already have?

This lifestyle isn't static–it's dynamic. And you're in control of every move.

Final Thoughts: The Hacker's Advantage

You don't need to spend more money.

You just need to spend with **intention**.

You don't need to work harder.

You just need to let your spending do some of the work **for you**.

You don't need to travel like a millionaire.

You just need to learn how to **travel like a credit card hacker**.

And now... you've done it.

You've joined a quiet revolution—one where your habits produce rewards, your credit opens doors, and your money works harder than it ever has before.

This is your system now. This is your power.

And your next free flight, hotel upgrade, or cashback win?

It's already on the way.

Congratulations. You're not just a credit card user anymore.

You're a credit card strategist. A reward earner. A financial hacker.

Now go live the life your points have earned.

Epilogue: What's Next on Your Journey

Thank you for listening to *Credit Card Hacking for Smart Borrowers*. If you're here at the end, you're not just someone who uses credit—you're someone who **leverages** it.

But this is only the beginning.

In the **next book in the Credit to Capital Series**, you'll discover:

- How to **legally dispute inaccurate or harmful items** on your credit report
- What your rights are under federal credit laws
- How to write **dispute letters that get results**
- And how to turn your clean credit into powerful financial leverage

That book is titled: **"Credit Disputes Masterclass: How to Dispute Negative Items and Win"**

It's your essential next step if you want to take control of your financial reputation, clear your credit history, and prepare for funding, homeownership, or business growth.

Listen now wherever books are available—including Findaway Voices, Spotify, Apple Books, and Audible.

And remember: every smart step you take with credit builds the foundation for something greater.

You've just completed one chapter of your financial transformation.

The next one begins now.

Other Books in the *Credit to Capital* Series

By Joe Correa

Unlock the full financial journey with these powerful and practical books in the *Credit to Capital* series. Each volume is designed to help you build, repair, and leverage credit to create wealth, purchase property, and launch businesses—no matter where you're starting from.

- **Book 1: How to Establish Credit in the U.S.**
- **Book 2: Personal Credit Repair Blueprint**
- **Book 3: How to Build Credit Fast Without Debt**
- **Book 4: Business Credit Mastery**
- **Book 5: Credit Card Secrets for Building Wealth & Rewards**
- **Book 6: Credit Card Hacking for Smart Borrowers**
- **Book 7: How to Leverage Business Credit to Fund Real Estate Purchases**
- **Book 8: Business Credit Ecosystem: Build, Stack & Automate Unlimited Funding Without Personal Risk**
- **Book 9: How to Get $1M in Credit and Keep It**
- **Book 10: Credit-Funded Wealth for Families**

www.ingramcontent.com/pod-product-compliance
Ingram Content Group UK Ltd.
Pitfield, Milton Keynes, MK11 3LW, UK
UKHW020158290926
15471UKWH00005B/941

9 798349 609633